SO-CBU-441

Growing
Shiitake
Commercially

Books by Bob Harris

Growing Shiitake Commercially

Growing Wild Mushrooms

Shiitake Gardening and Farming

OREGON

DEC 08 1987
STATE LIBRARY

DISCARD

Growing Shiitake Commercially

A practical manual for production of Japanese Forest Mushrooms

by Bob Harris

WITHDRAWN
East **From EOU Library**
La Grande, OR 97850

 **Science Tech Publishers**
Madison, Wisconsin

Library of Congress Cataloging-in-Publication Data

Harris, Bob, 1946–
  Growing shiitake commercially.

  Bibliography: p.
  Includes index.
  1. *Lentines edodes.* 2.Mushroom culture. I. Title.
SB353.5.L46H37 1986   635'.8   86-17784
ISBN 0-910239-07-X (pbk.)

Copyright © 1986 by Bob Harris. All rights reserved. Neither this book
nor any of its contents may be translated or reproduced in any form,
including electronic or digital means, without the written permission
of the copyright holder.

Science Tech, Inc., 701 Ridge Street
Madison, Wisconsin 53705, U.S.A.

Printed in the United States of America

10 9 8 7 6 5 4 3 2

Contents

Preface

Since 1982 when Dr. Gary Leatham first published an article about Shiitake as a potential forestry crop, interest in the cultivation of this mushroom has been increasing. In order to supply more information about the practicality of Shiitake cultivation I wrote a small booklet, entitled *Shiitake Gardening and Farming,* in the same year. However, there has been so much demand for more information that I decided to write this more complete book about growing Shiitake, which contains all the latest information that was available to me. Since writing this book I have had the opportunity to spend five more weeks in the Orient observing many different types of farms and obtaining detailed information about some of the practices that I observed. Thus one should view this book *Growing Shiitake Commercially* as the latest in a succession of books. I am now working on a new book which contains very precise information for cultivating Shiitake all-year-long in greenhouses using completely new methods.

In the United States the large commercial producers of mushrooms are now testing several methods of producing Shiitake mushrooms. Most growers here are using either pasteurized compost or sterilized sawdust medium. Compost has produced very poor yields to date, but sterilized sawdust medium has shown an impressive return of 110%–130% based on dry weight of medium. However this high productivity (in a relatively short cycle of about six months of fruiting) is partially offset by the high cost of producing the substrate and the high amount of capital outlay required for special equipment and specific growing conditions. Growers in Japan have traditionally rejected this method because they found that producing Shiitake mushrooms on whole oak logs is inherently cheaper. Taiwan currently produces 70% of its Shiitake mushrooms on sterilized sawdust medium. Although the industry as a whole is suffering from currently low market prices in Hong Kong and Taiwan, producers using logs as the medium are doing fairly well.

I believe that the initial interest in these artificial methods of production will stimulate the market; when the market becomes competitive the log method will ultimately succeed in the United States because of the overwhelming availability of the raw material: oak logs. Oak is considered a waste product in many American forestry areas. Utilizing this waste as a source of high quality food is my prime motivation for bringing to the American public as much information as possible about the cultivation of Shiitake. Once this information becomes readily available, I believe we will see many successful small-scale operations growing Shiitake all over the United States. It is my hope that these grass-roots operations will be able to compete successfully with the large commercial mushroom producers.

I would like to extend my appreciation to several people for their help in providing information and insight for me into the world of mushroom growing. Mr. Tahei Fujimoto has spent much time answering my many questions about Shiitake cultivation. Dr. Rolf Singer is always a source of inspiration for me and I value his friendship greatly. He above all other professionals understands the diversity of the concept of a professional mycologist. By classifying most of the edible fungi, the original publication of *Mushrooms and Truffles* served as the bible for most of us who wished to learn about Shiitake cultivation in Asia. Last but not least I would like to thank Professor George Carroll of the University of Oregon who served as my professor while I was in graduate school in Oregon. He inspired me to study fungi. Without his initial enthusiasm I probably never would have grown a single mushroom.

1

Introduction

Interest in the production of fresh Shiitake mushrooms in the United States has been increasing steadily in recent years. While Shiitake is a relatively new mushroom in the United States, it has been known for centuries in the Orient. Until 1972 Shiitake could only be imported into the United States in dried form because the live culture was not allowed into the country due to a Department of Agriculture quarantine. Apparently, the U.S.D.A. had confused Shiitake mushrooms, *Lentinus edodes*, with another species of the genus Lentinus, *Lentinus lepideus*, a fungus that causes rotting of railroad ties. Since the reversal of the quarantine there has been a steadily increasing interest in this mushroom, especially among home cultivators. With the appearance of more literature in the early 1980's, interest has focused on the commercial cultivation of Shiitake.

Most Americans are familiar with Shiitake as the black mushroom used in Oriental cooking. Recently many articles have appeared describing the culinary uses and possible health benefits of Shiitake. Today health-conscious and gourmet cooks all over the United States are cooking with Shiitake and the market for them is growing.

Shiitake mushrooms contain vitamins B_1, B_2, niacin, C, D_2 (ergosterol), and A; as well as the minerals phosphorus, iron, and calcium. The nonprotein matter contains trehalose, mannitol, pentosan, and methyl pentosan. The protein content of dried Shiitake is about 12 to 25% and the fat content varies from 1.6 to 2.5%. Notable amino acids are glutamic acid,

1

alanine, and leucine. According to Dr. Kanichi Mori, Shiitake lowers serum cholesterol, and has both strong antitumor and antiviral properties. In addition, Shiitake may stimulate the immune system and the production of interferon.

Shiitake, the most commonly accepted name for this mushroom, comes from the Japanese word which means "fungus of the Shii tree." In Japan, Shiitake occurs naturally on Shii trees, but they also are easily cultivated on oak species which are members of the same family. In China these mushrooms are known either as "Hoang-ko"[1], "Shanku"[2], or "Hoang-mo"[3]. Their scientific name is *Lentinus edodes* (Berk) Sing., having received their modern classification from Dr. Rolf Singer. A full description of the Shiitake mushroom can be found in the book *Mushrooms and Truffles* by Dr. Singer. According to his latest classification, *Lentinus edodes* is a member of the Polyporaceae, tribe Lentineae. It has a dark brown to light brown cap with a slightly reddish tinge; the younger caps are generally darker. The cap is often tufted with white scales, especially around the edges. The gills are white to off-white and may have reddish-brown spots when very old. The spore print is pure white and the stem is also white, although there can be reddish-brown areas due to age or bruising. When the cap is broken open the flesh is white inside (Figure 1-1).

The earliest date of cultivation of Shiitake in the Orient is unknown. Shiitake was praised as early as the year 199 AD by the emperor of the Kyushu district of Japan (still the area of the greatest concentration of Shiitake cultivation today)[4]. At that time Shiitake was gathered wild from rotten tree limbs. Methods of semicultivation probably began about 250 to 350 years ago in China and were refined in Japan. These early

---

[1]T. Ito, "Cultivation of *Lentinus edodes*" in *Biology and Cultivation of Edible Mushrooms,* Chang and Hayes, editors, page 461. New York: Academic Press, 1978.

[2]D. Kuo and Mau Kuo. *How to Grow Forest Mushroom (Shiitake),* page 1. Naperville, IL: Mushroom Technology Corp., 1983.

[3]R. Singer, *Mushrooms and Truffles,* page 138. London: Leonard Hill Ltd., 1961.

[4]R. Singer, *ibid.*

Figure 1-1 Shiitake mushrooms fruiting on an oak log. An example of the intermediate Koko type.

methods employed a system of spore inoculation in a natural setting: notches, called "Hodagi", were cut with hatchets on the felled tree trunks. The logs were then placed near logs bearing mature Shiitake mushrooms and exposed to their wind-borne spores. A refinement of this process used spores that had been collected on paper. The spore paper was then inserted into incisions made in the logs. At the turn of the century this technique developed into a method for using a suspension of spores in water as the inoculum. Spores to be used within a few days were collected in a suspension. If the spores were to be stored for later use, they were collected on paper and kept completely dry and cool. The disadvantage of this method is the high degree of variablity of the strains produced from spores, since the spores recombine each time they are produced, resulting in a new strain.

At the same time that the spore method became popular in Japan, another method was also in use. Older logs that were permeated with Shiitake mycelium were ground up and used as a source of "spawn." This spawn was then placed into fresh cuts in new logs. At the turn of the century, a variation of this method was developed by the Mori spawn company, in which the fungus was cultured on wedges of oak and then slipped under the bark of the logs to be inoculated.

While both the spore method and the nonsterile spawn method were an improvement over the "wait until the wind blows" method, they suffered from the disadvantage that the mushrooms produced were of variable strains. In the 1920's, K. Kitayima introduced the modern system of sterile spawn culture—a method similar to that developed for pure culture spawn of *Agaricus bisporus*. During the 1940's the Mori family popularized this method with the production of large amounts of sterilely grown spawn on oak wedges; this resulted in the true birth of the modern Shiitake industry in Japan. At about the same time, Tahei Fujimoto, a member of the Yamato Mycological Society, developed the modern plugspawn system which has become the most popular system today. In this method, holes are drilled in the log and inoculation is performed by inserting oak dowel plugs, on which spawn has been grown, into the holes. More recently, spawn cultured on a sawdust-nutrient mix has been substituted for the plugs because sawdust is cheaper and because the added nutrients allow a more rapid growth of the spawn. An even newer form, called "comb spawn", is now in use in Japan. This method employs the use of saw kerfs (slits or notches) in the log and the placement of wafers of wood (combs) impregnated with spawn into the kerfs. The combspawn method decreases the labor of inoculation dramatically, lowers the contamination rate, and accelerates spawn growth in the logs, thus decreasing the time until harvest. In this book we will thoroughly describe how to use both plug and sawdust spawn, as well as comb spawn.

A Note on the Photographs

Most of the photographs in this book were taken by the author in 1985 during a tour of Shiitake farms and research centers in Japan.

2

Choosing the Substrate

Shiitake mushrooms are grown on wood. Only hardwood logs can be used but they can be from a variety of species; usually oak, beech, maple, chestnut, and alder. For commercial cultivation, members of the oak family are the primary species considered. The tree species you choose, and the season in which the trees are felled will directly affect the success of your mushroom crop.

Suitable Tree Species

There are a few parameters to remember when selecting trees for growing Shiitake. Alder, beech, or aspen wood works perfectly well: in fact, Shiitake will actually grow a bit faster on these species than on oak and will fruit sooner if properly cared for. However, there are a few things of which the grower must be aware. First, the density of these woods is about one-half that of oak. Since the total harvest of mushrooms is related to the total weight of the log, one can expect to produce about one-half the amount of mushrooms from a log of these trees as from an oak log of the same diameter. The bark of these trees is also generally thinner than that of oak, and more easily damaged. Damaged bark can allow contaminants to begin growing. Thin bark also allows moisture to

5

evaporate more easily, so it is critical to watch the moisture content very carefully in logs of these species.

While it is difficult to compile a complete list of the tree species suitable for cultivation in the United States, it may be helpful to compare trees used in Japan with North American species.

The Japanese species listed below are taken from R. Singer, *Mushrooms and Truffles*:

OAK: *Quercus serrata, Q. acutissima, Q. crispula, Q. variabilis, Q. dentata, Cyclobalanopsis salicina, C. glauca, C. acuta, C. myrsinfolia*

SHII: *Shiia sieboldii* = *Castanopsis cuspidata* var. *Sieboldii, S. cuspidata* = *C. cuspidata*

CHESTNUT: *Castanea crenata*

ALDER: *Alnus firma, A. tinctoria, A. japonica*

MAPLE: *Acer pictum*

HORNBEAM: *Carpinus tschonoskii, C. laxiflora*

The trees most commonly used in Japan are *Q. serrata* and *Q. acutissima*.

According to Kuo and Kuo in their book *How to Grow Forest Mushroom*, the following trees are the best ones to use in North America:

OAK: *Quercus alba, Q. falcata var. pagodaefolia, Q. macrocarpa, Q. palustris, Q. borealis, Q. prinus, Q. velutina, Q. coccinea, Q. bicolor, Q. schumardii, Q. phellos, Q. lyrata, Q. michauxii, Q. imbricaria, Q. marilandica, Q. laurifolia, Q. nigra, Q. stellata, Q. virginiana, Q. garryana, Q. lobata, Q. chrysolepis,* (my addition: *Q. kellogii, Lithocarpus densifolia*)

IRONWOOD (HORNBEAM): *Carpinus caroliniana, Ostrya virginiana*

The following trees are of lesser quality; fast growing but short lived, according to Kuo and Kuo:

CHESTNUT: *Castanea species*

ALDER: *Alnus rubra*

ASPEN, POPLAR, COTTONWOOD, BEECH: *Populus tremuloides, P. grandidentata, P. balsamifera, P. deltoides, P. trichocarpa; Fagus spp.*

BIRCH: *Betula species except B. papyrifera.*

There are a few other kinds of trees that may be used but most are not of commercial interest.

Timing of Tree-felling

The logs should be cut green from living trees during the winter months while the sap in the tree is down. This insures the highest sugar content in the wood. Trees may be cut from the time that at least one-third of the leaves have turned yellow in the fall until the new shoots branch out in the spring. I am often questioned about the suitability of trees that are felled in the summer, since this is when most logging is done conveniently. However, the higher sugar content in the sapwood of winter-felled trees not only stimulates more rapid growth of spawn in the log but also results in a larger harvest.

On a cross section of a log, notice the physical arrangement of bark, cambium, sapwood, and heartwood.

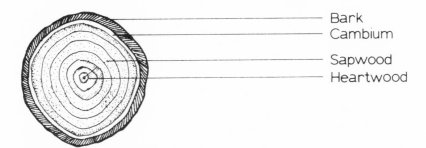

Bark
Cambium

Sapwood
Heartwood

The sapwood and the cambium are the areas within which the Shiitake mycelium will initially thrive. The mycelium spreads rapidly in a longitudinal direction within the cambium and sapwood, but grows at a slower rate *across* the log's diameter. Shiitake mycelium can digest the lignin in the heartwood, but will do so only as a second choice. The best growth occurs when the wood is high in the less complex celluloses and sugars contained in the cambium and sapwood. These substrates allow for rapid, expansive growth and provide the energy for later fruiting. In fact, fruiting can be correlated to the availability of these materials. Later in its growth cycle the fungus will attack the lignin in the heartwood which will sustain the fungus over the remainder of its life.

Cutting the Logs to Size

If there is a choice of several local hardwood varieties, especially in the oak family, pick wood that has a fairly smooth bark that is at least ¼ inch thick. A species with bark that is quite thin or easily removed is not desirable. (This is part of the reason why maples, as well as aspens and alders, are less desirable than oaks.)

Trunk sections of small-diameter trees are best, but branch wood from large-diameter trees can also be used. Branch sections should be straight, and free from any rot or twigs, while smaller (twig) branches should be cut off, leaving a stump approximately 2 inches long.

Combining the desirable factors of high sapwood content with smooth bark and straight lengths, the ideal is most often found in young growth, such as saplings and, especially, stump growth. In Japan, where the commercial industry is very competitive, the logs are cut from stump sprout growth every 8 to 15 years, depending on the regeneration cycle in the local areas.

Trees felled in the fall or winter for later use in spring can be left in whole lengths and cut to final log size when inoculation is done. It is important not to damage the bark layer in any way. Cut logs should be stored off the ground, away from direct contact with water or dirt. Trees felled in spring, for a spring inoculation, should be cut into final length immediately and inoculated soon after (Figure 2-1). The same is true for logs cut in fall for a fall inoculation (see Chapter 3).

Log Dimensions

A rule of thumb is that the number of years that a log will continue to fruit equals one year for each inch of diameter of the log. But the ideal size to work with is a 4- to 6-inch

Figure 2-1 Oak logs cut to length awaiting inoculation with spawn.

diameter log. Logs of this size also have a good ratio of sapwood to heartwood.

Many years ago, when I studied the only literature available from Japan, I read that logs must be 4–6 inches in diameter and 40 inches long. At first I could not understand why the authors were so emphatic about this. I have since learned that as far as the length is concerned, the 40 inch log was preferred solely because it can be carried comfortably by a man while longer logs are a bit too heavy. However, in more mechanized operations where a fork lift or chain hoists are used to handle the logs, a 48 to 60 inch length is common.

For the box method of incubation (see page 39), the logs can be as short as 6 to 12 inches or as long as 4–5 feet depending on the size of the box. The recommended diameter is still 4–6 inches for several reasons. While logs with diameters from 2–4 inches can be used and will yield mushrooms very rapidly, these logs decompose quickly and do not really afford much return for the amount of labor involved in inoculating them. Logs with diameters larger than 6 inches may be successfully used, but some drawbacks should be mentioned. Because spawn growth is slower across the radius of the log you must use more inoculations to compensate for the larger diameter. This requires more labor. In addition, because of its slower radial growth, the Shiitake mycelium will be slower to dominate the log. This increases the length of time until the first fruiting.

The major problem with increasing the time it takes the spawn to run through the log is that this greatly increases the chances that the log will become contaminated. Spending extra time to heavily inoculate a large-diameter log can mean a big loss if that log becomes contaminated. It is also harder to add water to a larger diameter log if it dries out. However, it is true that the larger diameter log will continue to fruit for more years. I have seen photographs of logs of 10–15 inches in diameter in Korea, that have been yielding mushrooms for 15 to 20 years, so if you don't mind waiting two or three years for the first crop you could consider trying large logs.

3

Preparing Logs for Inoculation

Curing the Logs

The traditional Japanese cultivation method includes a waiting period of 30 to 60 days to allow felled logs to cure before inoculation. Many growers have found that this period may be shortened and inoculate 7 to 15 days after felling. In fact, inoculation soon after felling may actually accelerate the growth of the spawn in the log as the higher moisture content of the freshly felled log is beneficial for spawn growth.

Most dormant, deciduous oaks have a moisture content at felling of less than 50%. Shiitake thrives when the moisture content is between 45 to 60%. Above this range growth slows; below 45%, growth also slows although it will continue fairly well. However, when the moisture content falls below 35%, Shiitake mycelium grows poorly. If you find that the moisture has dropped below 35%, water the logs prior to inoculation. It is important to water the whole log heavily for 12 to 24 hours and then let the surface of the logs dry using good air circulation. If you only sprinkle the logs a little bit every day, the water will not penetrate the bark and only the outside of the log will get wet. This will cause the unwanted growth of contaminants in the bark and will do nothing to help the growth of the Shiitake mycelium in the cambium and sapwood. The key point for the growth of Shiitake is to keep the inside of the log moist while the outside stays relatively dry.

Determining Moisture Content

There are two ways to determine the moisture content in your logs. You can measure it directly with a moisture gauge, such as those used in the lumber industry for determining moisture in drying lumber: an electrode is forced into the wood and the moisture content is read directly on the gauge (Figure 3-1).

If you do not have access to such a gauge use the second procedure: saw a small wafer of wood off the end of a log; weigh it, then dry it overnight in a warm oven left partially open (or until it stops losing weight); weigh it again; subtract the dry weight from the wet weight to get the weight of the

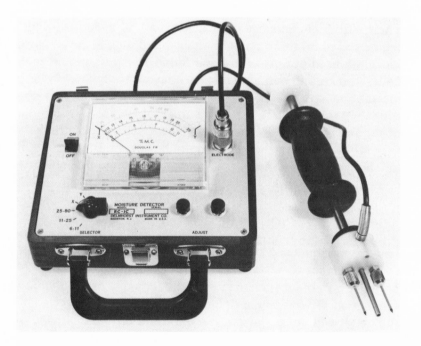

Figure 3-1 Moisture gauge for determining the water content of a log.

water in the wafer. The weight of the water divided by the wet weight of the wafer gives the percentage of moisture in the wafer, and by extension, in the log. For example:

$$\begin{array}{r} 120g = \text{wet weight} \\ -45g = \text{dry weight} \\ \hline 75g = \text{weight of water} \end{array}$$

$$75/120 = 0.625$$

Result: 62.5% moisture

$$\begin{array}{r} 100g = \text{wet weight} \\ -45g = \text{dry weight} \\ \hline 55g = \text{weight of water} \end{array}$$

$$55/100 = 0.55$$

Result: 55% moisture

Cleaning the Logs

Large amounts of lichens or moss covering the bark do not pose a *direct* threat to the Shiitake. They will affect the growth *indirectly* in a negative way as mosses and lichens will make drilling inoculation holes more difficult, more dirt will get in the holes as sources of contamination, and it will be difficult to keep the bark dry and free of contaminants. They can also make it more difficult to increase the internal moisture if you have to water the logs. Use a wire brush to clean these materials off the bark prior to inoculation.

4

Shiitake Spawn and Strains

Spawn

Shiitake spawn for commercial use is commonly available either as plugs made from hardwood dowels or as sawdust. Comb spawn, a new form, will be available soon. Each form has its own handling requirements, especially sawdust spawn (Figure 4-1).

All forms of spawn should be white, or white with brown areas when you receive it. Characteristic of Shiitake spawn is its fluffy white mycelium, with a distinctive browning reaction when exposed to light for a week or so. Shiitake also has a unique odor. Once you become familiar with the color and odor of healthy Shiitake spawn you will easily know when something is wrong with it.

After you receive the spawn, inspect it and smell it. Green mold is a bad sign, but Shiitake is fairly resistant to mold. If you are using plug spawn and find a few green plugs, discard the green ones, and the rest should be suitable for use. If more than 5% of the plugs in the bag have green mold, ask for a replacement. The same rule applies to sawdust and comb spawn. If the spawn has a very sour odor, the bag has been sealed too tightly for too long a time. Open the top seal slightly, reclosing it with a rubber band around a plug of sterile cotton to allow it to breathe. If the spawn still smells sour after being

14

Figure 4-1 Shiitake spawn in plug form.

open to the air for a week, it should be replaced. Do not let the spawn dry out—especially in the case of sawdust spawn—and avoid prolonged exposure to direct light.

Storing Spawn   Shiitake mycelium will grow at temperatures between 42° and 92°F and can survive between −50° and 100°F. Commercially produced spawn can withstand almost the same range, but I recommend that it be stored at 34–38°F if you must keep it for more than a month. Spawn stored at this temperature can be kept up to six months though it is best to use it within four months. At room temperature I recommend that it be used within two months.

If the spawn has been stored in the refrigerator or kept cold, bring it out and warm it to room temperature for at least two to five days before inoculating. This will allow growth to begin sooner following inoculation of the spawn into the log.

Testing for Viability   You can easily test the viability of the spawn at any point. Shake a few plugs or a bag of sawdust until the mycelium (whitish areas) seem to disappear. Place the plugs or a small bit of the sawdust spawn into a plastic bag containing a dampened paper towel. Seal the bag around a small plug of sterile cotton and keep it at a temperature of 75°F. The mycelium should become quite fluffy and white within two to five days. If there is no sign of growth after ten to fourteen days the spawn is not viable.

Shiitake Strain Types

Shiitake spawn comes in three basic strain types: cold weather, warm weather, and intermediate or wide range. Cold-weather strains fruit at temperatures between 40–65°F. Mushrooms produced by cold-weather strains have thick flesh and are considered the best grade. Warm-weather strains are heat tolerant and will fruit in temperatures from 50–80°F. These strains produce mushrooms which are less desirable because they have thinner flesh, and the caps open very easily. They require warmth for a good spawn run, and they usually fruit very well when the temperature is too warm for any other strains to produce mushrooms.

Each strain type generally produces a corresponding grade of mushroom. In Japan these grades are called *Donko, Koko* and *Koshin*. Donko have thick flesh with inrolled margins (Figure 4-2). Mushrooms of this grade are produced by cold-weather strains in cold temperature, low humidity conditions. Koshin are thin-fleshed with caps that tend to open up and flatten out easily. This grade is associated with warm-weather strains under conditions of high temperature and high humidity. Koko grade mushrooms are intermediate between Koshin and Donko, having medium, thick flesh and partially open caps. Koko are usually produced by wide-range strains or cold-weather strains under conditions of moderate temperature and humidity.

Environment and Grade   Environmental conditions can alter the type of mushrooms produced by a strain type, within certain limits. Under normal conditions you can expect Donko from cold-weather strains, Koko from intermediate strains

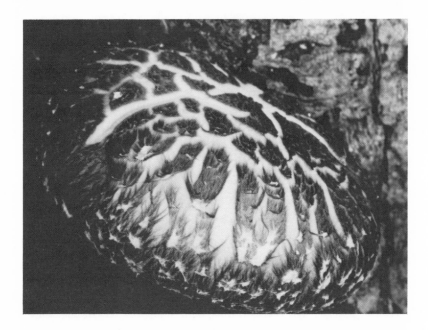

Figure 4-2 Highest quality Jo Donko Shiitake.

and Koshin from warm-weather strains. It is possible for cold-weather strains to produce both Donko and Koko mushrooms or for warm-weather strains to produce Koko or Koshin depending on the temperature and relative humidity. However a cold-weather strain is more likely to produce Donko mushrooms than any other strain. When ordering spawn it is best to select at least two types. For example, a grower in Arkansas would use a cold-weather strain for growth in the spring and fall, and a heat-tolerant strain in summer. This is true even when forcing the fruiting in greenhouses. The use of a cold-weather strain for fruiting in winter or a warm-weather strain in the summer reduces the amount of energy needed to maintain suitable greenhouse temperature.

5

Inoculation

Drilling the Holes

Logs are ready for inoculation when they have been cut to length, are dry on the outside, and free of dirt, lichens, etc. To inoculate with plug or sawdust spawn, holes are drilled in each log in a staggered pattern. Adjust the distance between the holes from 2½ to 10 inches to accommodate the length

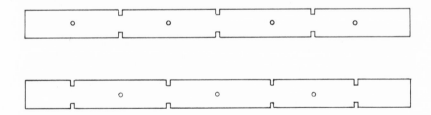

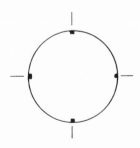

of the log. It is important to space the holes evenly so that the spawn runs uniformly in the log. Each spawn-filled hole becomes the center of a circle of growing mycelium that radiates outward.

Plug Spawn

This form of spawn is cultivated on wooden dowels ⁵⁄₁₆ inch in diameter by ¾ inch in length. An inexpensive plastic depth stop on a ⁵⁄₁₆ inch twist drill bit makes it easy to drill the holes to a uniform depth (Figure 5-1). Holes should be ⁵⁄₁₆ inch in diameter, and according to the latest research, 1¼ inches deep to create an air pocket below the plug (Figures 5-2 and 5-3). Hammer the plugs firmly into the holes and cover them with a thin coating of melted wax (Figure 5-4). The plugs must be slightly recessed below the surface and must not protrude.

Figure 5-1 Electric drill with depth stop.

Figure 5-2 Drilling inoculation holes in the log.

Figure 5-3 Multiple drill tool cuts four holes at one time in each log.

Figure 5-4 Hammering plug spawn into the inoculation holes.

Pierce Library
Eastern Oregon University
1410 L Avenue
La Grande, OR 97850

Sawdust Spawn

Spawn in this form is cultivated on a mix of hardwood sawdust and nutrients. Growers in the United States have avoided using sawdust spawn because of the difficulty of inserting the sawdust properly in the inoculation holes. This problem has been alleviated by the introduction of hand inoculation tools from Japan and Korea. The sawdust inoculation tool is essentially a plunger with a tube to hold the sawdust (Figure 5-5). The tool is forced into the sawdust spawn several times in order to fill the tube well (Figure 5-6). Then the tool is placed over the inoculation hole and the plunger is pressed to insert the spawn (Figure 5-7). The tool comes with an insertion tube of 1³⁄₁₆, 1³⁄₈, or 1⁵⁄₈ inches length for use with logs 4, 5, or 6 inches in diameter, correspondingly. Sawdust

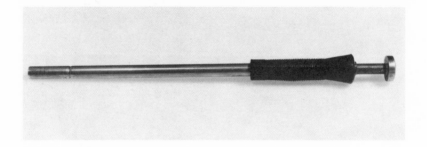

Figure 5-5 Inoculation tool for use with sawdust spawn.

Figure 5-6 Forcing the inoculation tool into the sawdust spawn fills the tube with a measured amount of spawn.

Figure 5-7 Inserting sawdust spawn into the inoculation holes.

spawn inoculation holes are generally ⁷⁄₁₆ inch in diameter; their depth depends on the diameter of the log. The spawn is then covered with a light coating of wax.

Because sawdust spawn costs about 35% less than plug spawn, it is economical to inoculate more heavily than when using plugs. Heavy inoculation accelerates spawn growth and usually results in an earlier first harvest while decreasing chances of contamination.

For Heavier Inoculation   If you wish to use heavy inoculation, drill three holes in the place where you would ordinarily drill only one. It is better to group them in sets of three across the circumference of the log because Shiitake spawn grows more slowly *across* the grain. Drill the holes in each set of three about ½ inch apart (Figure 5-8).

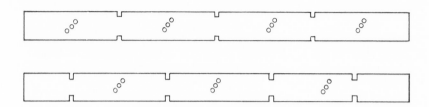

Figure 5-8 Pattern of holes for increased rate of inoculation with sawdust spawn to accelerate the spawn run and reduce time to fruiting.

Comb Spawn

A new type of spawn has been developed in Japan called *comb spawn* (Figure 5-9). Patents on the comb-spawn inoculation technique are pending in the United States for use of the method here. The concept developed from the practice of increasing inoculations along the radius of the log when using sawdust spawn. However, instead of drilling three holes, a saw kerf is cut along the arc of the log, and a "comb", or wafer, which has been cultured with sterilely grown spawn is inserted in the kerf (Figure 5-10). Only twelve wafers are required to inoculate a 40 inch log. The size of the cut and the dimensions of the comb vary with the diameter of the log. The combs are produced in five different sizes.

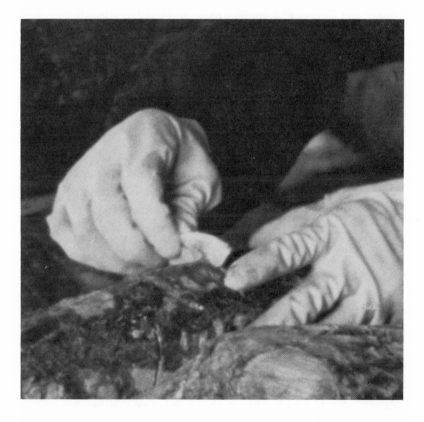

Figure 5-9 Comb spawn.

Figure 5-10 Inserting comb spawn into the log.

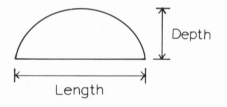

COMB SPAWN SIZE

Length (inches):	1¾	2⅜	3¹⁄₁₆	3¾	5⅛
Depth (inches):	½	¹¹⁄₁₆	⅞	1¹⁄₁₆	1¼

LOG SIZE

Diameter of log (inches):	2⅜	2⅜–3⅛	3⅛–4	4–4¾	4¾
Depth of sawcut (inches):	¾	1	1⅛	1½	1⅞

Sawtool for Comb Spawn   Three models of a mechanical sawtool have been designed with two, four, or six blades. To make 12 kerfs using a six-bladed model, six cuts are first made in one pass, then the log is rotated 90 degrees and the second set of cuts is made (Figure 5-11). The blades are activated by a foot pedal and the log is ejected onto a conveyor when it is finished. The combs are then inserted and waxed (Figure 5-12).

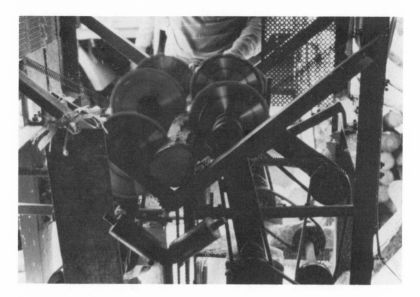

Figure 5-11 A six-bladed saw is used to cut kerfs in logs for inoculation with comb spawn.

Figure 5-12 Detail of comb spawn inoculation; notice how narrow the kerf is and the offset of the two cuts in the radial dimension.

A variation of the comb spawn-saw kerf method of inoculation for the hobbyist or home gardener is described in a publication of the Virginia Cooperative Extension Service[1]. A chainsaw is used to make the cuts in the log and sawdust spawn is placed in the saw kerf. The spawn is sealed with wax and the ends of the log are covered with foil. Tahei Fujimoto, a member of the Yamato Mycological Society and the developer of the comb spawn method, experimented with this method 20 to 25 years ago. He said the method was not as efficient as that using comb spawn because the width of the chainsaw cut required the use of much more spawn, thereby increasing costs. In addition, the wide cut contributed to a higher rate of contamination and loss of logs.

The Advantages of Comb Spawn

One person can inoculate about 100 logs per day using sawdust spawn. However, using the comb-spawn method one person can do about 300 logs per day. In Japan, inoculation is usually done in teams. I observed seven-man teams working with comb spawn: one person operated the saw, another fed the saw and cleared the inoculated wood, three to four people inoculated, and one or two people waxed the spawned logs. The increased speed of inoculating more than offsets the slightly higher cost of the spawn. Also, since only 12 combs are used per log the cost of spawn per log is lower. Inoculation with comb spawn results in much more rapid spawn growth which means much less contamination and a significantly earlier time of fruiting. When this type of spawn is used in conjunction with some of the new vigorous strains, one can obtain commercial fruiting within six months, especially using forced-fruiting methods in a greenhouse. A yield of about 2½ pounds per log can be achieved within two years after inoculation.

---

[1]Van T. Cotter, Tim Flynn, Rytas Vilgalys, and Andy Hankins. *Shiitake Farming in Virginia*, Virginia Cooperative Extension Service Pub. 438–012, November 1985.

Waxing

Wax is an ideal sealer since it breathes and keeps moisture in, and is harmless to fungi. Grafting compounds, on the other hand, often have solvent bases and may be toxic to fungi. A wax seal prevents water from evaporating from the inoculated holes, which would dry out and kill the spawn. Sawdust spawn is especially susceptible to drying. In drier climates it is good practice to also wax plug spawn. Water evaporating from inoculation holes may interfere with the normal conduction of water through the vessels of the wood. By using wax to seal the holes, the water in the log remains in the vessels. Little or no water will be conducted outward through the bark; instead it will pass through the vessels to the end of the log. Thus the fungus is also carried through the vessels as the remaining water is wicked to the two ends of the log.

Figure 5-13 Using a baster to wax logs inoculated with comb spawn.

You can use almost any type of wax—the cheaper the better, even paraffin. However, a hard wax such as paraffin often becomes brittle and flakes off. This is not much of a problem with plug spawn but sawdust spawn may fall out of the inoculation holes. To make the wax more pliable, I add up to 20% by volume of mineral oil (found in any pharmacy) to the melted wax. It is easy to melt the wax using a double boiler. The hot water in the double boiler also keeps the wax fluid while you are applying it. Use a small paint brush or a cheap flux brush for soldering to apply the wax. The wax can be applied very rapidly with a baster but you may have some problems with wax dripping out of the end. I have seen a glass baster in Japan with a slight bulb at the tip to prevent dripping (Figure 5-13).

6

The Spawn Run

Methods of Incubation

Once inoculated and sealed, the logs are ready for the critical phase—the "spawn run", or incubation period. There are two incubation techniques: the traditional method for commercial cultivation; and the box method for rapid small-scale testing, for year-round spawn run, or for incubating logs in adverse environmental conditions (very hot and dry-weather areas or very cold climates for a winter spawn run).

The Traditional Spawn Run

In the traditional method the period of incubation known as the spawn run occurs in the laying yard. The spawn run can take as long as one to two years depending on the strain, the temperature, and the environmental conditions. When conditions are optimum the spawn run can be as short as 4 to 6 months. The average in Japan is about 12 months with first fruiting at about 15 months.

Shiitake spawn can survive temperatures of −50°F and +105°F, but it will only grow between 40° and 92°F, with some variation for different strains. The optimum temperature for the growth of the spawn is about 72–78°F for most strains (see Appendix II, page 67).

In the laying yard, logs are stacked in such a way as to

prevent contamination and dehydration while the spawn grows through the logs. This is usually done by stacking the logs in a well-drained area under the shade of conifer trees or shade cloth (Figure 6-1). During the first year shading should be about 60 percent, while 65–70 percent is used after the first year. Special shade cloth has been developed in Japan which provides 60 and 70 percent shading while allowing the rain to penetrate.

The pattern used for stacking logs depends on several environmental conditions (Figure 6-2). Air must circulate through the stack so that the bark stays drier than the interior of the log, but not so dry as to cause evaporation of the internal moisture. The optimum internal moisture should be held between 35–45%, while the moisture content of the bark should be between 15-30%. Too much moisture allows green mold contamination to develop and too little will cause the growth of polypore-type fungi later.

You will need to experiment to determine the best kind

Figure 6-1 Natural conifer canopy used to shade the laying yard where Shiitake logs incubate.

Figure 6-2 Incubating logs stacked in an x-frame pattern on the slope of a hill.

of stacking pattern and spacing between the logs in order to achieve the proper moisture level in the logs. By monitoring the moisture in the log with a moisture probe and inspecting the bark you can obtain feedback about the results of different arrangements.

Temporary Laying

Immediately after inoculation the logs are generally arranged in a tight crib stack for a period of about two months. Tight stacking keeps the humidity high and the temperature constant to give the mycelium a good start. Since these conditions will also promote the growth of undesirable fungi, the tight stack is broken up after two months to allow more air to circulate. Greater air circulation promotes the growth of the Shiitake mycelium but not of competing contaminant fungi.

After a spring inoculation, shade cloth is usually put directly over the stack during the temporary laying period to prevent direct sunlight from drying out the logs.

Laying Yard Environments

After the initial two-month period the logs are stacked out in the final laying yard. If the laying yard is in a deciduous forest, shade cloth is put directly over the stacks during the months when the trees are dormant and without leaves. This cloth is removed in summer when the leaves are out (Figure 6-3).

When the logs are placed under the shade of conifer trees the stacking pattern is arranged according to the density of the canopy and the amount of air circulation in that location. The conifer canopy is created by cutting all the lower branches off the trees.

If the laying yard is in a valley under dense conifer where humidity is high, the logs should be stacked in a more upright position with ample space between them to provide air movement and lower humidity. On a high ridge under sparse conifer, such as tall pine trees, the logs should be stacked closer together and the stack laid close to the ground. If the laying yard is in a level area where winter temperatures are well

Figure 6-3 Stacked Shiitake logs covered with shade cloth incubating under deciduous trees.

below freezing and the wind is strong, there may be a freeze-drying effect that removes the water from the logs. In this case the logs should be stacked close to the ground, only one, or perhaps two, layers high and allowed to become covered with snow. This helps prevent freeze-drying. In addition, in areas with wind-chill effects, the laying yard can be surrounded with shade cloth hung vertically to prevent the wind from whipping through the yard.

Stacking Patterns

Three stacking patterns are commonly used in the laying yard: the x frame, the lean-to and the horizontal criss-cross. The x-frame pattern is used under denser conifers in valleys where there is little air movement. The stack is made with the logs in a vertical position and the x pattern keeps the logs fairly far apart to allow good air movement between each log (Figure 6-4). On slopes near the top of a hill the x pattern is less vertical with the logs closer to the ground.

Figure 6-4 A vertical x frame stacking pattern.

The lean-to pattern may be used near or at the top of a hill or under less dense conifers such as pine. Four to five vertical logs are braced against one horizontal cross log. This type of stack can be laid almost flat against the ground in areas where there is much air movement or sun (Figure 6-5).

On hill tops, and under an open conifer canopy with a lot of air movement you can also use a criss-cross stack. In this pattern four or five logs are laid horizontally in one direction and crossed by another four to five logs laid over them horizontally and turned 90 degrees (Figure 6-6). It is important to keep the incubating logs off the ground when using the criss-cross stack. This is usually done by simply starting the stack on two uninoculated logs placed on the ground and laying the inoculated logs across them. The criss-cross stack is relatively easy to maintain for first-time growers because moisture is easily kept in the logs. But this can present some problems since moisture on the outside of the bark will also stay high, increasing the chance for contamination. The stack

Figure 6-5 The horizontal lean-to stack, used under high, open canopy with light shade, such as pine; also in windy, cold weather areas.

Figure 6-6 The criss-cross stacking pattern for incubating or dormant logs in the laying yard under tall canopy of conifer trees.

must be in a well-ventilated area to allow for a chimney effect to circulate air around each log. Spacing for good air movement between logs should be at least 6 inches. With experience many growers prefer the lean-to method of stacking (Figure 6-7). The bark stays drier with this pattern, although one has to be careful that the logs do not dry out too much.

Artificial Shade

When using artificial shade during the temporary laying period the logs may be covered with muslin. Currently two types of special shade cloth are also available. One is made with rows of polyethylene spaced 8–10 inches apart, with streamers about 12 inches long which hang down allowing water to drip off. The second type of cloth is made of polyethylene strips that are gathered at intervals, rather than being woven.

Figure 6-7 The lean-to stacking pattern high up on a hillside.

This allows the rain to penetrate while blocking the sun (Figure 6-8). In the past farmers in Japan covered logs with rice straw for 40 days, and sprinkled the straw with water.

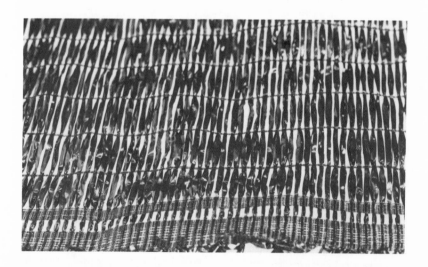

Figure 6-8 Special shade cloth designed to allow rain to penetrate.

Avoiding Contamination

If the moisture in the logs falls below the 35% level during the laying period you will need to water them. It is important to water heavily for a rather long period instead of several short daily waterings. For example, water the logs for 12 to 24 hours, then allow them to dry out on the surface for several days. This enables the water to penetrate to the inside of the log. Otherwise only the bark becomes wet and may cause contamination problems.

Green mold and polypore fungi are two common contaminants. If green mold appears during the spawn run, increase the space between logs to increase the air flow in the stack. Green mold can cause serious problems if it continues to grow. If it is caught early the contaminated log can be removed from the stack and further dried. The green mold will be killed and the log can then be returned to the stack.

The growth of polypore fungi is encouraged by rapid dehydration of the log, a result of the bark being too dry during the early spawn run because the log has been exposed to excessive direct sunlight or wind. Polypore fungi seem to have little effect on the production of Shiitake mushrooms, but they can cause the bark to deteriorate and thus interfere with the normal water regulation of the bark. (See Chapter 8 for a detailed description of contaminating fungi.)

The Box Method of Incubation

The box method can replace the spawn run in the traditional laying yard, including the temporary laying period. The advantages of this method are several. The spawn runs through the log faster when incubated in boxes. The grower has better control of the moisture content in the logs, and logs can be incubated year round. For example, in a heated barn the box method may be used for a winter spawn run.

In the box method, logs are covered with clean, dry cellulose material, and layered in cardboard or wooden boxes. Fruit bins make convenient boxes. If you plan to construct boxes do not use particle board or plywood in whole sheets because the resin glue used in the processing makes a solid vapor barrier. If you must use these materials either cut the sheets into slats or drill holes in them to allow air to circulate through the box.

The outer bark of the logs must be dry at the time of boxing. Place a layer of logs on the bottom of the box. Cover with fine, dry (less than 12% water content), clean, cellulose material. Use sawdust or rice hulls, for example, but avoid straw as it contains too many contaminating organisms. Cover logs with at least a half-inch layer of sawdust (or other cellulose material). Add a layer of logs and cover with sawdust in the same fashion. Add layers until the box is full. Seal the box and store it in a basement, garage, or under a porch, etc. It must be kept from direct sun, wind, rain, and moisture. Store it for four to six months, turning over (180°) every two months to ensure even distribution of moisture in the logs. In hot, dry areas inspect logs periodically for moisture content.

If your logs are at least three feet long, you can construct an artificial box with posts, wire fencing, and cardboard or burlap to use outside, but you must be able to keep it dry at all times. Since the best temperature range for incubation is 60–80°F, a spring or summer spawn run, in warm weather, is ideal for using outdoor boxes.

7

Fruiting

Four to six months after inoculation, inspect the logs. If the Shiitake mycelium has run completely and dominated the log, the ends of the log will be covered with white, fluffy mycelium. If this has occurred, move the logs from the laying yard to a more humid environment for fruiting. If not, return the logs to the stack or boxes for one or two more months. Remember that the white areas of mycelium will turn dark brown a few weeks after removing the logs from the stack. This is another indication that the Shiitake spawn has dominated the log. If other colors of fungal growth appear, then contamination has occurred, and the contaminated logs should be separated from the good logs.

Test for Growth

If the logs have been incubating for one year or so and there is no sign of mycelium on the ends of the logs, you may wish to check to determine how far the mycelium has run in the logs. There are two checks that you can do. One simple check is to take a small pen knife and dig around the inoculation points of either plug or sawdust spawn. After you carefully remove some of the bark you should be able to see white mycelium growing directly from the spawn into the sapwood. The mycelium will have digested this wood and changed its texture to a soft, fibrous, spongy texture. In fact this technique can be used at any time from four to six months after inoculation to be sure that the spawn is growing into the wood.

A second method is a bit more destructive but will be useful if you think that the logs may be ready for fruiting. Cut a wafer about one inch thick off the end of a log and discard it. Then cut off a second wafer, about ½ to ¾ inch thick, for testing. Place it in a jar or a plastic ziploc bag containing a small damp paper towel, that has been moistened and squeezed to remove any excess water. It is a good idea to seal the bag or jar loosely using a sterile cotton plug in the end which allows air to circulate while retaining moisture. After two to five days the wood should show fluffy, white growth on its surface. This could be either Shiitake mycelium or a contaminant, but once you learn the difference in the texture between Shiitake and contaminants, you will easily be able to identify the Shiitake mycelium. If you are just learning, you can test the mycelium further by exposing it to fluorescent light or sunlight three to five days after it appears on the wafer. Under these conditions the mycelium of Shiitake will become dark, chocolate brown in color within ten days to three weeks. Other contaminants, such as *Trichoderma*, will turn green. If the Shiitake has run well through the outer diameter of the sapwood of the wafer then the log is ready for the fruiting process.

Fruiting Outdoors

There are two major methods of fruiting: natural outdoor fruiting using seasonal rainfall or forced fruiting in a greenhouse. Fruiting outdoors occurs within two weeks after rainfall (Figure 7-1). While this is still the primary method used for the production of Shiitake, it is highly variable. Adverse environmental conditions can damage a fruiting and drought can inhibit fruiting altogether. In Japan year-round rainfall and adequate cloud cover during the spring and fall provide the right humidity and temperature levels for successful outdoor Shiitake fruiting (Figure 7-2). You will need to assess weather conditions in your area together with appropriate strain types to enhance your chances of a successful harvest.

Figure 7-1 Shiitake fruiting on an oak log.

Outdoor fruiting also creates problems for marketing mushrooms. When your mushrooms are fruiting in the spring and fall so are those of most other growers. However, the highest quality mushrooms, the Jo Donko, are produced outside. These thick-fleshed varieties have deep cracks or fissures in the cap, a condition known as *rimose* (Figure 7-3).

Figure 7-2 Shiitake fruiting outdoors on large oak logs.

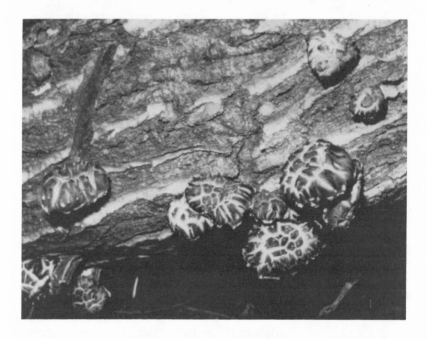

Figure 7-3 Highest quality Jo Donko fruiting outdoors in the spring. Notice the rimose pattern of the cap.

Mushrooms with this characteristic are most commonly produced by cold-weather strains (which fruit earlier at cooler temperatures). The mushroom forms when the weather is cool and moist. This is followed by warmer, drier weather which causes rapid growth and the subsequent rimose condition. This is the highest quality mushroom in Japan and will often sell there for up to five times the price of the lowest quality mushroom.

Stacking for Fruiting   The fruiting area should have somewhat more light and air movement than that of the spawn-run area. Shading, whether natural or artificial, should be about 65–70%. The logs must be protected from strong wind and direct sunlight. The logs are stacked outdoors in a pattern that allows for easy harvesting. The most common stacking pattern is the x-frame stack which is done in long rows up and down the sides of hills.

Greenhouse Fruiting

The second method of fruiting is in greenhouses under controlled conditions. This can be done all year long by controlling the temperature and humidity (Figure 7-4). However, the most successful growers generally fruit their logs in the greenhouse only during those periods when outdoor logs are not fruiting in order to take advantage of the best market. In Japan, the logs are prevented from fruiting in the spring and fall and are forced to fruit in the greenhouse during the winter and summer.

Greenhouses are made either of glass, or even better, of polyethylene film (Figure 7-5). There must be sufficient but not excessive light in the greenhouse. The ideal amount is generally said to be enough to read a book by; but this is hardly an accurate measure and the normal scientific methods for measuring light intensity is not available to everyone. I use the light meter of a camera as follows: set the film speed to ASA 400 and the shutter speed to ⅙₀ second. In optimum light the meter should read f4 when measured against a gray card or the back of your hand (Figure 7-6).

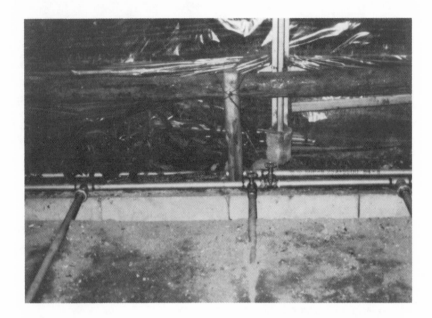

Figure 7-4 Pipes in the greenhouse floor for heating in winter.

Figure 7-5 Polyethylene greenhouse for forced fruiting.

Figure 7-6 Inside a greenhouse. Note shadecloth used to regulate the light.

The humidity inside the greenhouse must be at least 40%; the ideal is 60%. In winter old logs can be burned in a wood stove for heat. To raise the humidity inside a heated greenhouse, drip water onto the stove. Generally a greenhouse will hold at least two logs per square foot of floor space (including walkways).

Soaking   In a greenhouse, logs are soaked by submerging racks of logs in tanks (Figure 7-7). Racks are typically made of welded channel beam or pipe (Figures 7-8 and 7-9). An alternative construction method uses rebar rod bent into a rack (Figures 7-10 and 7-11). The logs are soaked until the internal moisture level reaches 50%. The duration of the soaking and the temperature of the soak bath vary according to the season. In general the water temperature should be about 9–11°F cooler than the air. Since it is harder to create this temperature difference in the winter, the soak time will last as long as 2–4 days (Figures 7-12 and 7-13). In the summer it is easier to create the temperature difference, so the soak

Figure 7-7 Placing racks of Shiitake logs in soaking tanks with a forklift.

Figure 7-8 Soaking racks made of pipe. Racks are moved with a forklift.

Figure 7-9 Soaking racks made of steel box channel.

Figure 7-10 Rebar soaking rack.

Figure 7-11 Shiitake logs in a rack made of rebar ready for soaking.

Figure 7-12 Soaking tanks.

Figure 7-13 Circulation pipes in the soaking tank for controlling the water temperature.

period may be as short as 6 hours. The following temperature differences require the following soaking times:

Temperature Difference (°F)	Soak Time (Days)
2–4	3–4
5–8	2
9–12	0.5–1

Some growers aerate and circulate the water which may decrease the time necessary for soaking. Heating or cooling of the water may be necessary to create the necessary temperature differentials.

Shocking the Logs   After soaking, the racks of logs are removed from the water after draining the tank. The logs are then "stimulated" which produces larger yields or "flushes", by physically "shocking" the logs. Usually this is done by placing the racks on a vibrator that shakes them at 1850 rpm for 30 minutes (Figure 7-14). An alternative method is to hit

Figure 7-14 Vibrator for shaking racks of Shiitake logs after soaking to stimulate fruiting.

the rack against a steel plate. Researchers are currently investigating the use of lightning to stimulate fruiting.

Stacking for Fruiting in a Greenhouse   After shocking, the logs are moved into a greenhouse and stacked for fruiting. Generally the logs are set in a compact stack and covered with damp muslin for four to five days to induce as many mushroom pinheads to form as possible. Some growers create high humidity by keeping the logs inside the empty but covered tanks for four days in summer or six days in winter. In either case the logs are then stacked in the final pattern for fruiting.

Several different kinds of racks are used for stacking the logs for fruiting. The simplest stacking patterns merely lean the logs up against a rail with the butt down on the ground (Figure 7-15). More sophisticated racks permit horizontal placement of the logs on many tiers, making use of the vertical height of the greenhouse (Figure 7-16). Another method requires placing the logs on special racks on a gravel floor in a dense pattern. By stacking the logs two per square foot on the floor higher humidity is maintained (Figure 7-17). The special racks allow harvesting by moving the slope of the logs in the opposite direction (Figure 7-18). It is a cheap system, and more effective than the metal-frame shelving racks.

Figure 7-15 Simple method of stacking logs on the ground inside the greenhouse for fruiting.

Figure 7-16 Fruiting logs stacked horizontally on racks inside a greenhouse.

Figure 7-17 Racks for concentrated stacking of fruiting logs on the ground inside a greenhouse. Beams extend from a rail fastened to the wall to rebar stanchions (see next photo).

Figure 7-18 Racks shown in previous photo with logs set in place to show how they are flipped forward for harvesting mushrooms.

Harvesting and Resting   Depending on the strain, the log diameter, and the methods used, the harvest life of a log usually varies from one to three years and can be fruited between five and eight times during this cycle. The harvesting period lasts about 10 days so fruiting logs are inside the greenhouse for about 14 days and then new logs are brought inside. At the end of the fruiting sequence, or *flush*, the logs should be moved from the greenhouse to a rather dry environment for at least 20 days (until the moisture content drops below 35%) before resoaking. Most farmers use a one- or two-month rest time between soakings (Figure 7-19). During this dormant period the logs are kept under shade cloth and covered with a bamboo mat to keep off rain. The logs are stacked on a vertical slant four or five to a row with a horizontal cross log between rows. The stacks are about 4–5 feet wide and about 100 feet long. If the temperature difference is very great between indoors and outside when the logs are moved out of the greenhouses into dormant stacks, cover the stacks with muslin for one week.

Figure 7-19 Logs stacked outside after fruiting for a rest period before repeated soaking and fruiting.

Fruiting is induced when natural harvests do not occur and inhibited during the time of seasonal outdoor fruiting. Logs are inhibited from fruiting by *dead stacking* (compact stacking with logs all parallel and little or no space between them) and then covering the stack. This reduces changes in temperature or moisture content in the logs. By inhibiting fruiting during the natural harvest time, larger harvests are produced during the off season when the market price is better. At the end of the fruiting sequence, or flush, the log can be allowed to dry slightly for several months and the fruiting cycle repeated. This cycle can be artificially induced in greenhouses up to four times a year for one to three years depending on the diameter of the log. It is especially important, however, that the bark be treated with care and kept intact. At the end of its harvest life the log is discarded and a new log is inoculated. By inoculating several batches yearly one can have continuous fruiting.

Fruiting with the Box Method   Using the *box method*, mycelium should have grown through the log in six months. Inspect the logs periodically for contamination and to see if the spawn has grown out the ends. Generally, contamination occurs only if the log was not thoroughly dry when it was placed in the box, or if the sawdust was wet or became wet during the four-to-six-month incubation. The logs I have done in this fashion have shown no contamination and all had Shiitake mycelium grown throughout.

Fruiting Procedures

The logs can now be prepared for fruiting. Initially the logs should be soaked for 24 hours under water. For example, they can be submerged in a garbage can or a tub of water. They should then be stored for one or two months in a cool, moist environment that has either indirect light or fluorescent lights (cool white or grow-lights). If the logs are small (6–12 inches long) they can be kept in a bucket with moist sand on the bottom. If the logs do not fruit during this time, they should be allowed to dry slowly over the next two to three months—

until the logs feel lighter. At this time they should be placed in a cool environment for eight to nine days (such as in a garage, outdoors in spring or fall, or placed in a refrigerator). They should then be soaked for 24 hours under water.

Within a week the first mushrooms should appear. If not, repeat the cycle of slowly drying out, storing in a cool area, and soaking.

Harvesting

The mushrooms are ready for picking when the cap expands and the veil pulls away from the stem. They are removed with a twisting motion. The mushrooms can be used fresh or dried in a food dehydrator for later use. In most cases, all the mushrooms will ripen at approximately the same time or within a few days, which is called a flush (Figure 7-20).

Figure 7-20 Young mushrooms emerging from logs which had been soaked for fruiting in a greenhouse.

8

Pests and Contaminants

Pests

Relatively few pests attack Shiitake. Probably the most serious predators are slugs. They are best dealt with by using bait or ashes around the growing area. If you are cultivating outdoors you may simply prefer to ignore them. Keep the ground around the stacks free of the weeds and grass which harbor slugs. Bark beetles sometimes attack the logs but this is rare. If the weather is wet, warm, and humid, and there are lots of mushrooms present or stems left on the logs, mushroom flies can breed. Insects can be controlled effectively by the use of Pyrethrin sprays. These natural pesticides are effective yet are relatively non-toxic. Do not use directly on the crop; spray between flushes if possible. Apply pesticide with a fogging apparatus using a cold fog. Be sure to wear a protective mask when handling these pesticides. The need for pesticides is generally very minimal as Shiitake seems to have its own built-in insect repellents.

Competing Fungi

The more serious problems for cultivation of Shiitake arise from the fungi that compete with them or attack the logs. Most notable among these are:

Trichoderma viride and *Penicillium* spp.—these are the common green molds and are the most frequently encountered contaminants when the bark is kept too wet. These fungi are white at first, becoming green to blue-green or yellow-green as they mature. If they are caught early enough, they can be easily controlled by simply removing the log from the stack and exposing it to more air and light, i.e., generally drier conditions. If the entire stack has green mold, restack it with more space between the logs and put the stack in an area that has more air movement. If the green mold is allowed to grow it will eventually destroy the log and prevent any Shiitake from developing. One note: if the Shiitake mycelium has developed to the point where it is present in at least 85% of the log it can overcome any green mold.

Hypoxylon coccineum appears initially in the form of small black dots in the grooves of the bark. It eventually develops into hard black pustules in the bark. Generally this fungus enters the wood prior to inoculation and its growth can be prevented by keeping the bark of the logs dry before inoculation. It is especially prevalent when logs have been dragged through water-soaked ground or left on the ground for a long period of time before inoculation.

Schizophyllum commune is a common small fungus with a white or light gray, fan-shaped fruit body covered with dense whitish filaments or hairs. It has no stalk. The white tissue is thin and leathery with prominent gills radiating from the attachment to the log. The gills are white to off-white. It is found on the dry surface of the Shiitake logs, mostly on areas that have been exposed to sunlight. It seems to have little effect on the growth or production of Shiitake but generally indicates a condition of too much sunlight or dryness in the bark.

Coriolus (Polystictis) versicolor is a pernicious fungus that infects the Shiitake logs. It grows in layers that resemble stacks of tiles. The surface is soft, velvety, and filamentous, with circular patterns of yellow, red, green, or black on a gray background. The tissue is white and leathery. It is rarely present the first year after the log has been inoculated and is found in sunny but not well-ventilated laying yards. It grows well in areas of high temperature and humidity.

Cryptoderma (Hypocrea) citrinum is found in high-moisture conditions and forms colorless conidiospores, which form flat spots with age. A relative, *Hypocrea shweinitsii*, grows well in drier areas. This fungus can cause severe damage, rotting the log and preventing the Shiitake from growing. It appears in the form of green or yellow-green spots which change color to green, dark green, or light brown to dark brown.

Merulius tremellosus, lacrymans is seen on the surface of the bark as flat, soft, yellow-brown to red-brown wrinkled spots. It grows well in high humidity and can destroy the logs. If the bark is kept dry it will not grow.

Poria vaporaria, versicora appear as white spots along the bark, and if allowed to develop forms a dense tissue. The tissue is corky and becomes leathery when dried, and is easily peeled from the log. Generally this fungus develops from contact with the ground and is a potent cause of wood rot. It is more prevalent the second year and is very pernicious, destroying the Shiitake fungus.

Lenzites betulina is a gray-white, shell-like fungus. It starts forming in layers with short hairs on the surface of the fruiting body. Like *Schizophyllum*, it is not generally harmful but if it is allowed to develop it can reduce the yield of Shiitake. It will not grow in areas that are well ventilated.

9

Drying Shiitake

Shiitake may be sold either fresh or dried. Wholesale prices for dried Shiitake vary between $20 to $50 per pound depending on quality. Shiitake fresh from harvesting are from 85–90% water depending on season. When sold dry, their moisture content is usually 10 to 14%. Thus, approximately seven pounds of fresh Shiitake yields one pound of dry mushrooms. If they are dried much more they become brittle and are likely to break apart when handled. Once dried they should be stored in a cool, dry environment (Figure 9-1).

The best method for drying Shiitake is to use a lower temperature at first, followed by increased heat. Sun-dried mushrooms contain vitamin D_2, whereas those dried with hot air do not. However forced-air drying is more rapid than sun drying or uncontrolled drying and produces a stronger flavor than that which is found in even the fresh mushroom.

The vitamin D_2 content in dried Shiitake can be increased with artificial fluorescent lighting with a spectrum of 280–320 nm, the near UV-spectrum[1]. Research showed a better result with artificial light than with sunlight, in part because artificial light does not damage or destroy the other vitamin

[1]Tadayoshi Ono, Kunitaro Arimoto, Kyoichi Kano, Kengo Matsuoka, Wataru Sugiura, Hanji Sadone, and Kisaku Mori. "Vitamin D_2 Formation in *Lentinus edodes* (Shiitake) by Irradiation with a Fluorescent Sunlamp." In *Mushroom Science IX (Part 1), Proceedings of the Ninth International Scientific Congress on the Cultivation of Edible Fungi,* pages 435–443, Tokyo, 1974.

Figure 9-1 Dried Shiitake packaged for marketing.

B complexes. Irradiating the gills proved 10 times more effective for production of the vitamin as irradiating the pileus (cap) and irradiating the stipe (stem) was more effective than the cap. This may be due in part to the increased surface area of the gills over the smooth surface of the cap. The amount of irradiation necessary was 30 E-viton min/cm². At the stated levels irradiation with artificial light on fresh mushrooms for 10 minutes seemed sufficient.

For drying mushrooms, gentle heat is used first (90°–100°F), and the temperature is gradually increased to 140°F as indicated below.

Time (Hrs)	Temp	Vent In	Vent Out
0–2	95°F	Full Open	Full Open
3–4	104°F	Full Open	Full Open
5–6	113°F	⅓ Closed	⅓ Closed
9+	122–131°F	½ Closed	½ Closed
Final Hour	140°F	Closed	Closed

If the mushrooms are harvested during the rainy season, a longer heating time is required for drying as follows:

Time (Hrs)	Temp	Vent In	Vent Out
0–2	86°F	Full Open	Full Open
3–6	95°F	Full Open	Full Open
7–8	104°F	⅓ Closed	⅓ Closed
9–12	113°F	⅓ Closed	⅓ Closed
13+	122–131°F	½ Closed	½ Closed
Final Hour	140°F	Closed	Closed

Dried mushrooms contain from 6 to 10% water on removal from the drier. They are hygroscopic and may contain 10 to 13% at the time of sale. If the moisture reaches 20% the caps lose their sheen.

Appendix I
Production Numbers

A cord of oak logs, each of which is 36–40 inches long × 3–4 inches in diameter, contains approximately 250–320 logs. A light inoculation of spawn uses about 30 plugs per log, so a cord of wood will use about 10 bags of spawn (1000 plugs per bag). If it is purchased in large quantity, the spawn will cost about $150. The equivalent amount of sawdust spawn costs about $100.

In one day a team composed of 3 to 5 people can inoculate up to 125 logs per man. In Japan, for example, a team of four men can routinely inoculate and wax 500 logs every day. One cord of wood will produce about 2.5 pounds of mushrooms per log over the life of the log whether the mushrooms are forced in one year or naturally flushed over 3 to 4 years. This means a yield of about 550 to 750 pounds of mushrooms per cord. At a wholesale price of $4 per pound this can mean a net return after costs of about $2000 to $2500 per cord. These are very conservative numbers since the wholesale price is often higher, especially when fruiting is timed to coincide with the high market. These figures can change somewhat if cultivation is accelerated using either of the following methods:

1. Indoor Spawn Run Using the Box Method.
A box measuring 4 × 4 × 2 feet (32 cu. ft.) will hold 20

logs. A building 10 feet high, with a floorspace of 80 × 80 feet will house 2,000 such boxes (64,000 cu. ft.), or 40,000 logs per year. If half of the logs are done in the spring and half in the fall then a building 10 × 40 × 80 feet is needed.

2. Forced Fruiting of Logs in the Greenhouse.
A greenhouse 75 × 150 feet (11,250 sq. ft.) will hold 10–12,000 logs, or one log per square foot. After soaking, each batch of fruiting logs will occupy the greenhouse for about two weeks. The greenhouse can therefore handle about 25 batches, or 300,000 logs, per year. If each log is forced to fruit four times a year, then 75–100,000 logs must be inoculated each spring to achieve continuous production.

If forced in a greenhouse, the life of a 36–40 inch log with a 4 inch diameter is 1–2 years. The yield per year is 50–100% of the total, or 1.25–2.5 lbs. per year. If 75,000 logs are in production, then approximately 95–190,000 lbs. of mushrooms can be produced per year. This is the result of using the highest speed methods and the fastest spawn type available. Using lower inoculation rates and cooler temperatures may require twice the length of time to generate the same figures.

Appendix II
Shiitake Strain Data

The following tables illustrate specific characteristics of various Shiitake strains. The strain numbers are the stock numbers assigned by their producer, *Mushroompeople*. A free catalog of Shiitake strains, growing supplies and literature is available from: *Mushroompeople*, PO Box 159, Inverness, CA 94937.

SHIITAKE STRAINS SUITABLE
FOR VARIOUS ENVIRONMENTS

Cold Weather	Warm Weather
841	512
854	852
855	853
858	

Greenhouse		Wide Range
82a	853	82a
510	854	510
841	855	851
851	858	
852	859	

STRAIN DATA SUMMARY

Strain No.	Fruit Temp	Soak Temp	Temp Range	Greenhouse
851	50–82°F	<68°F summer	Wide Range	Yes*
852	50–86°F	<73°F summer	Warm	Yes
853	50–82°F		Warm	Yes*
854	41–65°F	<62°F winter	Cold	Yes*
855	41–65°F		Cold	Yes*
841	45–68°F	39–55°F	Cold	Yes*
858	47–68°F	39–68°F	Cold	Yes*
859	50–77°F	55–73°F	Warm	Yes
510	50–75°F	50–75°F	Wide Range	Yes*
512	50–77°F		Warm	No
82a	50–75°F	50–75°F	Wide Range	Yes*

*Can be grown outdoors or in the greenhouse.

Additional Reading

Books and Pamphlets

Forest Mushroom Cottage Farming *Lentinus edodes*. Toby Farris. Asheville, NC: Toby Farris; 1982. 11 pages.

Growing Shiitake (*Lentinus edodes*) on Logs. R. Kurzman. Berkeley, CA: Kurzman's Mushroom Specialties; 1982. 4 pages.

Grow the Japanese Forest Mushroom Shiitake *Lentinus edodes*. Gilberto R. Garcia. Arcata, CA: Gilberto R. Garcia; 1980. 8 pages.

How to Grow Forest Mushroom (Shiitake). Daniel D. Kuo and Mau Kuo. Naperville, IL: Mushroom Technology Corp.; 1983.

How to Grow Oak Tree Mushroom—Shiitake. Byong W. Yoo. College Park, Md: Dr. Yoo Farm; 1976. 12 pages.

Is Shiitake Farming for You? Rick Kerrigan. Goleta, CA: Far West Fungi; 1982, revised 1983. 22 pages.

Manual of Oak Cultivation. Eung Rae Lee. Seoul, Korea: Korea National Federation of Forestry Association; 1980.

Mushrooms as Health Foods. K. Mori. Tokyo, Japan: Japan Publications; 1974.

Shiitake Farming in Virginia. Van T. Cotter, Tim Flynn, Rytas Vilgalys, and Andy Hankins. Virginia Cooperative Extensive Service, Publ. 438–012; 1985. 10 pages.

Shiitake Gardening and Farming. Bob Harris. Inverness, CA: Mushroompeople; 1981, revised 1983. 14 pages.

Chapters in Books

Ito, Tatsuziro. Cultivation of *Lentinus edodes*. In *The Biology and Cultivation of Edible Mushrooms*. Chang and Hayes, eds. NY: Academic Press; 1978, pages 461–473.

Singer, R. The Shiitake and its Cultivation in East Asia. In *Mushrooms and Truffles*. London: Leonard Hill Ltd; 1961, pages 132–146.

Tokimoto, K., and M. Komatsu. Biological Nature of *Lentinus edodes*. In *The Biology and Cultivation of Edible Mushrooms*. Chang and Hayes, eds. NY: Academic Press; 1978, pages 445–459.

Magazine and Journal Articles

Cultivation of Shiitake, the Japanese forest mushroom, on logs: a potential industry for the United States. Gary F. Leatham. *Forest Products Journal* 32 (8): 29–35; August 1982.

Cultivation of the Shiitake Mushroom. James P. San Antonio. *Hortscience* 16 (2): 152–156; 1981.

A Fungus Fit for a King. Joseph Alper. *Mother Earth News* 86–87, September/October 1980.

The Ginseng of Mushrooms. S. MacLatchie. *Organic Gardening*, November 1978.

The Healing Mushroom Shiitake. J. Belleme. *East West Journal* 11 (12): 49–52; December 1981.

Gourmet Mushrooms Faster. Warren Schultz Jr. *Organic Gardening* 29 (11): 51–55; November 1982.

Shiitake Cultivation in Japan. Bob Harris. *Mushroom Journal* 10 (4)–1: 25–29: Winter 1985–1986.

Shiitake News. South Eastern Forest Resource Center. Lanesboro, MN. 1984–present.

Shiitake: the $20 per pound (or More!) backyard crop. Mary Alice Krebs. *Mother Earth News* 38–41; January/February 1986.

Spawn Disk Inoculation of Logs to Produce Mushrooms. James P. San Antonio and P.K. Hanners. *Hortscience* 18 (5): 708–710; 1983.

Newspaper Articles

These farmers hope that demand will mushroom for fancy fungus. Michael Days. *Wall Street Journal*; October 11, 1984.

Move to US-grown Shiitake mushrooms may lower prices. Carol Flinders. *The Oregonian*, Portland, Oregon; November 29, 1985.

Index